Doomsday

The 9 to 5 Man's Guide

To Bug-Out & Survival

Written by Tom Redford

Thomas Redford was born in Marseilles, a small town in Illinois, in 1953. He is the only son of Ray and Sara Redford, and has one older sister Janet Applebee. Thomas graduated from Marseilles High School in 1972. He was an average student, but dreamed of being more and becoming a Science Fiction writer someday. He spent his teenage and most of his adult years working at the local Paper Mill at Nabisco Inc. During this time he also owned and operated a small local tavern call Yardbirds, a nickname he was given as a young boy, which still sticks with him today. He moved to Dallas, Texas in 1985 where he attended DeVry University. He was on the Dean's List and the Presidents List during his 3 years while attending DeVry. After graduating from DeVry, and attending North Lake Collage, he went to work for the Offshore Company, Western Geophysical, based out of London, England where he traveled all over the World. To places like, Malta Italy, Bayonne France, Morocco, Venezuela, and Argentina, just to name a few. During this time period is when Thomas started doing much of his writing while out on the ocean for long periods. He had always had a passion for Science Fiction and History, and had even been interested in becoming a History Teacher at one time. Therefore, he decided to combine both his passions and become a fiction writer.

I wanted to write this book in hopes of helping other people like myself, that feel something will happen in their lifetime to this World that we all are so comfortable living in. This book is especially geared for the average person that has thought about trying to get prepared for when the SHTF (shit hits the fan) but really does not know where to start. I feel that I can pass on some good knowledge of what a family can do to protect themselves when something does happen. I do not believe we will have a Zombie Apocalypse, but I do feel that the way the world has been going something will happen in the near future. Whether it is an EMP pulse, some type of virus outbreak, a third world country launching a nuclear attack or a solar flare, something will happen. Now I am writing this book mostly for anyone that lives in the city, but people that live out in the country can also use my suggestions. However, whatever goes down, and if you happen to live in the city, you will have to get out ASAP.

That does not mean everyone jump in the car and head out with a few supplies. Because you will not survive. In addition, depending on, what happened when the SHTF, your vehicle may not even run? I will explain what steps you need to do to give you and your family a fighting chance to start a new life. These ideas are not set in stone, but they are an excellent guideline to get you started.

If you follow my suggestions in this book, they will give you the stepping-stones and a head start compared to other people that have no idea how their life will change, and are not prepared for whatever type of problem hits our world. I do not go into detail on things like how to build a shelter step-by-step, building trap for wild animals, or setting up a power source. The reason being, if I did this book would be excessively big to absorb the information that you would have to read. I do list some books that will tell you everything you need to know on how to accomplish those few things. The books that I list are generally not very many pages and inexpensive, plus some of them are laminated so you can use them on the trail. Now, there are a ton of books out there telling you how to become a Doomsday Prepper and how to abandon your lifestyle, by getting completely off the electrical grid, raising livestock, storing up food to last for years, and fortifying your home. Now there is nothing wrong with these types of books and life style if a person wants to commit to it. However, this is no easy task because most people nowadays all have colored TV, gaming systems, Internet, and going to the local store when you need something.

However, to get a better understanding of what I am talking about, compare yourself and your new lifestyle to the early pioneers, living off the land for everything you need to live. If you tried living off the grid all the time. So this is why I wrote my book the way I did, I just wanted to give people a head start on their new lives. Unbelievably, there seems to be an order of events that will follow no matter what happens. First, we see people that think our Government will fix everything in a few days. Then there are the party people that think it is Mardi Gras time and no laws apply. Next up looting, and then after people realize that no help from our Government is coming, then the panic starts to set in. Riots, major property destruction, and then you will start hearing gunshots through the day and night.

By this time, it will be a dog eat dog type of life style, especially if you are still living in the city. Mainly because when people start to panic they get very desperate when they are hungry, and thirsty so they could be your best friend thanking you with a pat on your back one day, then putting a bullet in your head the next day for a piece of bread. If you have waited this, long before thinking about leaving the city your chances have reduced drastically to making it out alive. This does not mean everyone jump in the car and head out with a few supplies.

Planning ahead

First off, you will have to decide where you are going to bug out. You will then need to get a map of the State you live in, and the area you will be bugging out too. Then follow these few steps to make sure you survive to see another day.

Step 1: On your map mark where any Nuclear Plants are located, then mark where any Military bases are located. This would also include any National Guard Bases. Then mark where any Major Hospitals, but depending on what happened when the SHTF you may want to stay away from Hospitals, because chances are they will be overrun with people. I also suggest getting a topographical map to show what kind of terrain you might encounter, this map should also show you most of the major waterways, rivers, lakes, etc. I would suggest getting them laminated so they do not ruined during your trip.

Step 2 Decide where you will be going and map out a route. The NRC, **(Nuclear Regulatory Commission)** suggests 120km about 75 miles is a relatively safe distance to stay clear of a plant if there is a problem, **(now of course this also depends on which way the wind is blowing and how hard it is blowing.)** The bottom line is, stay as far away as you can. Doctors will tell you that you need to drink at least 2oz of water a day to stay alive, and of course, this depends on your activity. However, you can only last about 3 to 4 days without water before you start to get very dehydrated. As for food, they say you can go 4-6 weeks without eating, (but again this also has many variables in it, depending on your activity), so you will have to plan accordingly based on the distance you will be traveling and the terrain you will have to walk through.

Everyone should have his or her Bug Out Route planed ahead of time, so when you have to bug out you know exactly where you will be going. Take a day trip and go out to the spot you have picked out. Now, seeing how you are only doing this for practice you can drive your car some of the way if you site is a long way to get too. By doing this road trip ahead of time you will be able to see how much trouble it will be to get there and get a general idea of the time it will take to get there without getting lost, plus you can work on reading a compass. It takes the average person 13 minutes to walk a mile, now there are many variables that will play into this. A few examples are the terrain, person's body size and shape, and temperature of the day, so you will have to plan according on how long it will take you to get to your bug out site.

Bugging Out

You have to keep in mind you will probably be doing a lot of walking, so you will need to try and keep the weight and amount of your supplies as small and light as possible. Another thing you are going to have to commit to is that you are willing to do anything you have to do to keep yourself and your family safe even if that means killing someone that is trying to kill you, or turning down people that are begging you for help or food. I know that sounds cold-hearted, but you have to remember you are trying to save yourself and your family.

That is why it is much safer to keep out of sight as best as you can, and, if you start seeing other people and ask them to join your group that will just be more mouths to feed. Like I said earlier people get very desperate when they get hungry, so they could be thanking you with a pat on your back one day, then putting a bullet in your head the next day for a piece of bread. Now, depending on how many people are in your group **(the smaller the better,)** and you are hiking through the woods heading toward your campsite there are a few things you need to do to keep safe. Make sure you are spaced out a little so if any shooting starts you will not shoot each other in their backs, plus it will be harder for the people that might be shooting at you to take out your whole family.

Before you start out walking, you need to come up with some type of code if someone sees something out of the ordinary, or thinks the family is in danger. Something like coughing two or three in a row or a catchphrase something like "boy it's pretty out here." That way everyone in the group will know to take cover and form into your battle strategy. This should be decided before you even start out walking. Now a few short suggestions about walking, depending on where you are going, you could be doing a lot of walking. Therefore, you will definitely need a good pair of walking boots and heavy socks that you have previously broken in. Also depending on each person's physical shape, you will need to keep handy some medicine from your first-aid bag. Foot powder, anti- fungus cream, and Band-Aids will be necessary.

Reason being if someone is a little out of shape they can develop a yeast infection on inside of their legs and possibly arms and if not taken care of. This can become very serious and even cause death when the bacteria works into their system and poison their immune system, so this is where the anti-fungus cream will come in handy. In addition, you will have to pay close attention to your feet; you need to make sure you try to keep them as dry as possible with powder on them. In addition, if you can wash them every other day and try to keep clean socks on you will be better off. Now this will really apply if you have a long distance to go but if you only have to travel one or two days you could probably get by with one change of socks. But again all these rules are subject to change depending on a person's body and physical shape.

Just a short note about Pet's, now I have pet's myself, 5 cats and 3 dogs well it bothers me to say, but I am afraid they are on their own. I have a German Shepherd that I will take because she is trained, so unless you have a good size dog that is very well trained, and you feel it will help you protect your family in the end. They will have to stay behind, they will only slow you down, and could possibly give your position away if someone hears them barking, or sees them, plus you will have to bring food and water for them.

You're Outfit

All the clothing I list should be the Army Type Outfits **(the reason being that they more durable than regular clothing and camouflaged)** and like I said earlier you could not trust people. Therefore, you are much better off staying out of sight of other people, and having camouflaged clothing. You will need heavy work socks, and good pair of hiking boots **(make sure you have broken them in way in advance)**

Weapons

There is a Golden Rule Concerning Firearms Safety First. You have to make sure whoever is using a firearm that they know how to handle it, cleaning it, and shoot it safely. Moreover, speaking of firearms if someone confronts you and you draw your gun on them you had better have it set in your mind to shoot them before they shoot you. Just holding up a gun and pointing it at someone to try and scare them is not what firearms were meant for, they were intended to protect you and if the other person is a very bad person they will probably shoot you DEAD. Now I am not saying to draw your gun and shoot them before you or they even have a chance to say anything, I am just saying be prepared to take a life. This is not easy thing to do but if it comes down to either you or him, you will need to choose yourself.

Here is a sample of what weapons I carry, but depending on what your taste is for firearms, you can chose whatever you like.

Good tactical leg holster for your sidearm, (this way your waist will be clear so you can carry a canteen and possibly your machete, or your hatchet) 9mm with three 13 round clips, 22 magnum revolver with three speed loaders. An 12-gauge pump shotgun 18" barrel with the plug pulled out, 14 ½" survival combat hatchet, 23" machete, 13" tactical knife, and a 8" pocket knife. In addition, a good tactical vest that way you will be able to carry your spare ammunition clips, your speed loaders, some shotgun shells, knife, and possibly another Sidearm. I know some people may read this and think I am going overboard and getting ready for a war. However, when the SHTF there is going to be mass panic in the streets and the chances of getting help from the Police Force or the Government will be very unlikely, so it is every man for himself.

Bag 1

A good backpack **(here are some general dimensions)** padded shoulder straps, 100% nylon, 28"x16.5"x11.8", at least 5 separate compartments, 2 survival blankets, camouflage netting, at least a 3 man tent. A couple of good flashlights, extra batteries, collapsible hand saw, water proof matches, several flint's, several bags of magnesium fire starter, rain poncho, wool blanket, sleeping bag, survival rope **(something small for things like tying up a tent brace or hanging things in tree's or other small job's.)** A couple of snare kits **(for trapping small game,)** fishing kit, a few plastic bags **(assorted sizes,)** good knife sharpener, a few candles. At least a dozen Ladies Tampons **(used for fire starting,)** gun cleaning kit, small army shovel, 2 compass's, good binoculars, climbing rope, assorted Zip-Ties, **(All the clothing should be camouflage,)** three pairs of army pants, 3 pairs of good work socks, 3 pairs of underwear, and a good hat. This is just a general idea of what to carry, and could be split up into two bags.

Bag 2

This backpack does not have to be a very big one; it does need to have several pockets on it though. Good pair of scissors, pair of tape scissors, 2 pairs of good tweezers, magnifying glass, bag of wooden tongue depressor's, **(all kinds of uses for these, splints, etc.,)** Q-tips, several box band aids, gauze pads **(numerous**

sizes). Several gauze rolls, several rolls of medical tape, aspirins, neosporium, anti-itch cream, few bottles of alcohol, anti-fungus cream, few bottles of hydrogen peroxide. A couple tubes of sunscreen, couple tubes of hand lotion, few tubes of lip balm, couple bottles multi-vitamins, couple bottles of vitamins C, scalpel, several wound closures, antacid pills, couple bottles of iodine **(this can also be used as a water purifier.)**

Bag 3

A lot of companies sell survival food in resalable buckets but I like a backpack because it is easier to carry plus I like to put together my own food; it is a lot cheaper. Now of course you cannot pack enough food to last for months and months, so this list is just to try to get you through for maybe one month if you ration it properly. Mess kit silverware included, couple of water bottles, can opener, small coffee pot, small cooking mess kit, water purification kit, power milk, dry soup, rice, bouillon cubes, salt, sugar, peanut butter, instance coffee, several Power bars, olive oil, several cans of Spam, several cans of Vienna sausage, and several packs of beef jerky.

Hydration Water Backpack, (option)

They make these and are inexpensive, but in my opinion, they do more harm than good in a situation like this. Because you have a tube running from the backpack up to your mouth where you can take a drink very easily and it is a temptation to keep drinking. In addition, in a situation where you do not have a good source of water and will have to conserve water for a few days, you could end up drinking all your water up in no time at all.

Setting up your Campsite

You need to try to follow some of these suggestions when you plan on setting up your camp, if it is only a few days since you bugged out and you are still fairly close to any towns, or a few houses. Of course depending how many people are in your family you may need to set up an armed look out during the day and night. If you are by yourself, you are just going to have to try to stay hidden as best as possible. The best scenario is finding a cave to live in, but depending on the State you live in that may not be possible. Make sure your site is on as level ground as you can find in case you have bad weather, your campsite will not be washed away. In addition, if you are planning to do much cooking and fire building you need to make sure your fire pit is not right under a tree. As for your fire pit you need to dig it about 5 to 8 inches deep, then put some fairly big rocks in a circle around it at least 2 or 5 inches high that way you can lay a grate on top of it to hold your pots and pans while cooking.

On the other hand, if you have a big pot you want to hang and cook stew or something like that in you really need to have three pieces of some type of heavy metal pole about 1 to 1 ½ inches in diameter. On the other hand, you can always use tree branches like you see them doing on TV but you have to make sure and change them out regularly so your pot doesn't fall in the fire. However, whether you going to use the fire for cooking or just setting around it at nights you want to keep the fire as low as possible to cut down on the smoke. You need to make sure you only use good dry wood and not any green wood **(green wood will give off smoke)** the reason being you can see smoke a long way off.

Now if this is your permanent campsite and you have eaten all the canned food that you brought with you and are going to have to start relying on any food that you killed or trapped. You will need to remember clean and dress any game you get away from your campsite preferably where you shot it or trap it and make sure you bury all the guts from your kill. When you get your meat back to the campsite it will have to be salted and hung up to dry, **(and you have to make sure to hang it up high enough so animals cannot get to it.)** This is where one of the books on how to preserve your food will come in handy. You also have to remember to make sure you do not leave any food scraps laying around your campsite when you are eating because it will only attract wild animals.

Going to the restroom and getting rid of garbage are two very important things to keep in mind, when you have to go to the restroom. You need to stay a couple hundred yards away from your campsite whether you are just urinating or having a bowel movement you have to make sure to bury it, or this will attract wild animals also and start to smell eventually at your campsite. I know it sounds petty when I say bury your urination but if you are going to be in the area for a while it will eventually start to smell. For this, I generally kick a little hole in the dirt and then kicked dirt back over the top of it, as for your bowel movement I bury that at least 5 inches deep it is best to move around and do this in several spots.

In addition, it is always best when you leave the campsite to have someone with you and both be armed, if you have to go by yourself make sure you are armed and looking out for anything. As for cleaning utensils, clothing, and bathing it is always nice to have your campsite near a waterway. Hopefully you can find a waterway not too far away and just transport the water back and forth. I have also listed a book how to build a shelter, and how to fortify a shelter, but you definitely need something to keep you out of the weather.

Now I did not mention it earlier when I talked about putting together your bug out bag, but not knowing what the future will bring there are a lot of things you could do to help you if you are setting up for the long run. First off, you really should have a bug out campsite located this way you can really get ahead of the game. Because your main food, supply will only be what you can hunt, trap, and find growing wild so my suggestion is to buy some bags of seeds like, cucumbers, squash, green beans, sweet potatoes, white potatoes, sweet corn, and carrots. Then vacuum pack them in some bags and you can either put them in a small plastic bucket, but make sure to seal the bucket good then go bury them on your bug out campsite but make sure you have a map of where you buried them. On the other hand, some people just like to carry them in their bug out bag after they vacuum seal them because they do not take up much room. There is also a lot of talk about setting up your home in a cave, or in the side of a hill. Here are two safe places to stay out of harm's way, but they do have their down falls.

Number One; if you build in the side of a hill, you have to make sure you build a back escape route out of you home in case of a fire or attack from someone or some animal. You will also have to put in a chimney pipe for cooking, also one or two vent pipes for oxygen, and of course, you would have a door, or something to seal off the front entrance.

Number Two; now if you decide, and are lucky enough to find a cave make sure no animal lives in. If it is something like a mining cave that has been abandoned, or the minerals have run out all the better, but that being said you do not want to go exploring all through it. I would go back only as far as you feel safe but you have to make sure you have plenty of light and you are looking at the celling & walls very- very good for signs of a cave in, and as with the home in the hill side you need another exit out of the cave. Now with the cave, this may not be possible because like I said you do not want to go exploring all through the cave, so you will have to decide if you want to take the risk of not having another way out. Also talking about the chimney, and the vent pipe this would be very hard to do so this would be another decision you would have to make if you want to live in a cave.

Books that will help keep you alive to see the Future

Here is a list of books that will come in handy when you bug out, you do not have to get these particular book titles, but you would need some type of books referring to the same subject matter. You can get most of these books off the internet or from Amazon, they usually are small around 50 pages or less so, they will not take up much room. The books in **red** really need to be with you when you bug out, while heading to your bug out campsite. The other books are more intended for looking toward the future if whatever caused the problem in the world is going to last for some time.

- ➢ Power from the wind achieving energy independence.
- ➢ Build your own solar power electricity from the sun.
- ➢ Guide to fortifying your retreat.
- ➢ Edible plants.
- ➢ How to navigate with a compass.
- ➢ How to build a shelter.
- ➢ Plant that heal, nature medicine.
- ➢ Outdoor knots and rope work.
- ➢ Trapper's bible.
- ➢ Water 4 You.
- ➢ Cooking outdoors.
- ➢ How to preserve wild game.

- Skinning & Tanning working with Pelts, Fur, & Leather.

- Ham Radio for dummies.

- Garden Wisdom everything you need to know to plant, grow a garden.

- Back to basics (A complete guide to traditional skills).

Some good general tips for surviving in the outdoors.

- Do not trust anyone, people will do the worst things you can imagine, and things you cannot imagine when they are hungry, desperate, and in fear for their family.

- If you need to make a fire, start out with some very small twigs and a few leaves, then open up a Ladies Tampon, spread out the cotton end of it, and put it in the middle of the twig ball. It should be about as big as a hardball. The Tampon will take right off when a spark hits it, you might need to blow very lightly on the base of the fire to help it catch the twig ball. I always carry about a dozen Tampons with me for this purpose.

- For some coffee on the trail, I will put enough coffee in a white handkerchief then tie it up so it is a ball. Them all you have to do is drop it in a pot of water you are cooking over a fire or outdoor stove. I only leave it in the water until it is strong enough for me then I take it out and let it dry so I can use it again **(only about 3 times)** because the longer you leave it in water the stronger it gets.

➤ Now of course depending on how long this breakdown of our world continues, money may not be worth anything for quite some time, if it ever is again. So people will have to survive as they did back in the Pioneer days they will have to either work for someone to get something that they want from that person, or start trading things with other survivors. Some people stockpile Gold but that gets to be expensive, and who is to say that Gold will be worth anything, I would assume it will still hold its value but you never can tell.

➤ Now depending on what has happened to the world and your water situation is running low, and if you have access to any abandon building and the people have left without draining their hot water heater you can usually find some water left in theses.

➤ When building a fire to keep warn, or for cooking, try to see what way the wind is blowing, and put up what they call a windbreak. Say for instance the wind is blowing North move back about 2 to 3 feet away from your fire and build a little fence about 3 feet wide and about 2 to 3 feet high on the North side of your fire. You can build this out of fairly big tree branches or even rocks. This way it will keep the wind from blowing on your fire, and reflect the heat back on you.

➤ Everyone should have sleeping bags to sleep in when they are camping, but if you are, unlucky to have one you can always dig down about 2 to 3 feet in the ground, then lay some small tree branches down, and then pile some brush on top of the small branches. You then can lay a blanket on the brush, that way it will be a little softer than the hard ground. You can then pile some leaves and real small brush on top of you to stay warm.

➢ Using this same idea, if it is cold out you need to build a nice fire and get some rocks and set them by the fire and get them nice and hot. You then bury them in the bottom of your hole and cover them with dirt, then lay some brush on top of the dirt and this should keep you warn for a while.

Setting up a Permanent Living Co-op and forming a Coalition

A co-op is a collective of people who have organized to form a jointly controlled company or village, which meets a specific need, such as housing, provision of food, and so forth. Now depending on what caused the breakdown of the world you may be looking at a few months before the Government becomes organized, or it could take years. The Native Americans lived in tents their completely. However, it is a lot safer and more comfortable living in a sturdy built cabin. There is a lot of truth in the old saying "there is strength in numbers" So forming a partnership and Coalition will take a lot of work, but it may be worth it. **(I could write a whole book on forming a coalition, but my best suggestion is get a copy of how to do it and keep it with you for future references)** but depending on how long the breakdown will last you will need other people around you to survive, here are a few suggestion than might help you get started.

- ❖ First off, you would need to form a Board, and you will need the Board to be respected by all members in your group, so that everyone will take the Board's decisions seriously.

- ❖ You will have to make sure you have enough key players on Board so that those left out cannot block progress.

- ❖ The Board needs to develop trust in one another and a shared goal so that they can make the needed change happen, no matter of any resistance they meet.

- ❖ The most important aspect of a Coalition Board is Diversity. An effective Board should be comprised of individuals in your group who will bring unique skills, experiences, perspectives, (this would be things like a person that has been a Trapper, someone that knows a lot about electricity, a carpenter, a couple of Doctors preferably one that has worked with Home Remedies, a plumber, and a teacher). This will allow the Board to see all sides of an issue and enable the most innovative ideas to solve any problems and come up with new ideas to improve the Coalition.

Now setting up permanent housing like this is going to take a lot of work and a fair amount of land to build everything needed. First off, if you have outside groups that are violent and are out there to take advantage of the weak you will have to make sure you have armed guards around the clock guarding your village. Now a lot of doomsday peppers groups have talked about taking over a building and fortifying it instead of building something up in the wilderness. This will all depend on where this building is located at and what type of building it is. You would definitely not want one with a lot of entrances and exits, because that would be too hard to defend. I am on a couple of doomsday peppers websites and they talk about looking at small prisons, National Guard buildings, and small airports with huge metal buildings, now of course these all would have to be deserted. However, depending on what actually happened to cause the world to go to HELL, will play a big part in deciding what type of living arrangements you choose.

There could be a power issue also because depending on what kind of shape the world is in so you may not have a power grid to access, so you are going to have to come up with your own power system. Which could be a combination of solar power, and wind power but again setting this up will depend on what you could find. Now setting up something like this would definitely be a lot easier if a Coalition group was up and running, or at least a group of 4 or 5 people working on it that know something about doing this **(I have also listed a few books on setting up power).**

Important Note

Seeing as how I will now be talking about some electronic equipment, you really need to have a Faraday Cage. Now for some people that do not know what this is, they are something that will protect your electronic equipment from an EMP pulse and they are very reliable, NASA use them. You can buy

premade bags and cages, or if you prefer you can make your own which are relatively easy to make. You keep all your electronic in it so an EMP pulse will not destroy them.

Here is some extra equipment that will come in very handy if it looks like it will take months or even years to get our country back up and running. Some of it is very expensive, and some of it is cheap enough to buy right now. Some of it would be nice to buy and have in your bug out bag right now if you can afford it; Night vision goggles, Dual Band Two Wave Handheld radios, handheld GPS unit, satellite phone, and a solar panel battery charger. Once you have set up a permanent location, a CB Base Station will come in very handy, by letting you hear any type of CB radio talk of other people that may be around your area. In addition, depending on what happened to the world, the GPS units and the satellite phones may not work. If there are no satellite circling above us, but losing all our satellites would be a long shot, now their orbit may degrade but it will take some time for that to happen, so you may still have use of them for a while.

THE END or THE BEGINNING.

I hope that I have set your mind at ease somewhat in how you can get started in preparing what to do when our world has some type of catastrophe. This next section I will be going into will give you a greater and more detail information about protecting your home if you decide to stay in the city, building a compound, raising livestock best suited for your needs, water needs, fire starting, Apocalypse bunkers, and growing your own food. I hope you enjoyed the first part of my book and will let your friends and neighbors know about it so that we all can survive and try to get through our life journey.

YOU'RE YARD

First off, if you do not have a fence around your property you will need to build one, at least 6 to 7 feet tall. This next step you may want to do this at night when there is no one around to watch you. You will need at least a 2 inch wood screw, and you will need plenty of them, then standing on the outside of your fence you will start screwing them in at least 1 ½" to 2 " down from the top of the fence facing into your house and at least 2 to 3 inches apart. This will keep anyone that tries to climb over you fence something to think about when they tear their hands up. Next you will need some pieces of plywood at least 10 to 12 inches wide, and how ever long you want, because you will be putting this on the ground all along the inside of your fence. You can either drive 4" nails or use 4" screws and put them through the plywood, when you are done they will be laid on the ground with the nails or screws facing up in case someone jumps over your fence, they will be very sorry. **Now do not put these out unless the other people around you start to panic and begin looting, or worse yet you start hearing gunshots throughout the day and night. In addition, if you feel that you have to defend your family and property.**

FORTIFYING YOUR HOME

Now the improvements that I will be talking about may sound very drastic and sort of like you are preparing to go to war. However, if you are serious about staying in your home these improvements will help you survive. To start you will need to use at least 3 sheets of ½ to ¾ inch plywood, or at least 5 to 6-inch diameter tree logs and attach them to the inside wall of your house from the floor up to at least a 4-foot height. These will be somewhat of a bullet-stopping barrier. Now of course if you have access to metal sheeting that would give you more protection. However, if you do not, the plywood or tree logs will be at least some protection. Then cut out at least 3-gun slot's per side of your house spaced out along the length of the wall, with a metal plate covering each slot that you would be able to slide off to the side so you could shot out of the slots. Make sure these are at the top of your bullet-stopping barrier. You also need to make wooden shutters that you can cover your windows with, made out of the ½ or ¾ inch plywood that I talked about earlier, and hang them on the inside of your house above each window.

You would hang them so you could just slide them down over the window if needed, with gun slots cut in these also. When talking about the bullet barriers you could get by with just putting them facing the front and rear of your property. Because that is where most assaults from the enemy would be likely to be coming from.

A PREPPERS COMPOUND

Now some of the ideas I am getting ready to tell you about will take some time to build, it will also be easier if you have access to some heavy equipment, like tractors or end loaders. If you decide to start building a compound before the world goes to hell, you might want to consider putting up a perimeter wall made out of concrete, or if you have access to a rock quarry, you could even use huge rocks. If you have decided to get out of the city and are planning on building a compound, the ideal spot for your compound would be near some sort of water access, but if that is not possible you will just have to bring water into your compound by hand.

You could also build your perimeter fence out of trees that you will cut down and pile up all around your compound. You should try to make it at least 5 to 10 feet wide and 6 to 8 feet high. Then dig a trench around 3 to 4 foot wide and about 3 to 5 foot deep somewhere around 8 to 10 feet away from the inside of your fence. A good idea is to put sharpen sticks on the bottom of the trench, so if someone was to fall in they would be impaled on the sticks. Your house that you will be staying in should be at least 50 yards away from your perimeter fence so you have a good size-killing field, that way if the people attacking you get over your fence you will have time take most of them out before they reach your house. In addition, if you see you are way out number you will have time to retreat if needed.

POWER FOR YOUR COMPOUND

Now depending what has caused the world collapse you may not have access to electricity, so that means you are going to have to make your own. Every house in the world should have a generator no matter what is going on in the world, even in good times. However, that also means that you will need gasoline, propane, or diesel to run your generator. In addition, when the world shits itself you may not have access to these fuels. There are a few alternatives for making your own power; but it will come down to how much money you are willing to spend. There is Solar, Wind Turbines, and Water Powered Generators. I will not go into each of these because I could write a whole book on each one. Therefore, I would suggest that whatever one you decide that you might want to set up, you get yourself a few books on how to set up a system.

LIVESTOCK

Depending what happens in the world there will be a food shortage, so fresh meat may be hard to come by. **Rabbits** now these animals would be more suited for you if you decided you were staying in your house in the city. First off get some chicken wire and tack it to the bottom of your fence and bury it under the ground in a u shape at least 24" wide on the inside of your fence. If you follow this plan, by burying the chicken wire under your fence the rabbits will not be able to dig out of your yard and you will be able to have meat all the time. Now you will need to get yourself some rabbit's at least two males and two females. These rabbits will be able to provide your family with meat all year long. The main reason I am telling you to get rabbits is they do not make noise, like chickens, goats, or cattle, so they will not attract attention. In addition, other people that have no food source will not see them. In addition, they will pretty much live by just eating the grass in your yard, so you will not need to worry about buying food for them. Now you will have to keep the males and females separated, and in cages until you have your yard set up so they cannot get out, plus that way they cannot start breeding.

Goats now some people may be think about getting some goats for milk or a meat supply. While this is, a good thought because like rabbits you really do not need to worry about feed for them because they will eat grass also. They need a lot more room than rabbits and they will eat a lot more grass. In addition, they will make a lot more noise and draw more attention, but if you were living on a compound this would be no problem. However, if you are staying in the city rabbits are your best bet.

Now I will not go into a lot of information on raising some of the bigger livestock like, cattle, and horses other than to say these will take a fair amount of land, housing, feed, and bedding. First off, you will need to make sure you have fencing around your property so the cattle or horses do not get away and to protect them from other people. You will then have to make sure you check them each day. Of course, you will also have to have a barn on your property so you can have a place for them at nights and raising their young if, you are going that route. So as you can see this type of livestock means a lot of extra land, and work force.

GROWING YOUR OWN FOOD

Now if you are planning to stay in the city and depending on how big your yard is you may want to plan a spot for a little garden. Now you will have to take all the grass up so that whatever you plant grow. Next, you will have to plan accordingly to where you want your garden to be, because you really do not want it to be visible from the street or the other houses around you. Now if you were using rabbits as a meat source you would have to fence in your garden so the rabbits will not eat all your vegetables. To make sure you grow a good garden you will want to think about fertilizer, which means having a compost pile.

Now the next part I tell you about may turn a few people off, but remember your life may depend having food to eat when there are not stores around to go buy your food at plus farmers having been doing this for many years. ***Human Waste:*** First off, you will want to keep the compost as far away from you house as you can. When the world gets to this point when everything has collapse you probably won't have working plumbing so you will be using some sort of outhouse or at the minimum a plastic bucket.

After you have gone to the bathroom in your bucket, **(urine, waste, and toilet paper, it can all be used.)** You will need to have a compost pile, after you deposit your waste you will cover it with a layer of dried leaves, or shredded brown pine straw, or dried grass clippings. You should use approximately the same amount of covering material as human waste. This will keep the odor under control and it will help keep the heat trapped inside the compost pile. Rinse or clean the toilet bucket and then return the empty toilet bucket to its normal location inside your home. Then immediately wash your hands.

Other Compost Pile Materials that that could be added to the compost pile include crushed egg shells, fruit and vegetable peels, used coffee grounds and filters, used tea bags, kitchen scraps, apple cores, fireplace ashes, shredded junk mail, shredded cardboard, garden weeds,. Always chop or shred any large items into smaller pieces. It is good idea to build a big box with a cover to help hold the heat in and cut down on the smell, now you will have to stir and mix up the compost every 4 or 5 days to get some good compost.

WATER NEEDS

As for keeping the garden watered and coming up with drinking water for yourself depending on if there is any water running after the world collapses you may have to come up with finding your own water supply. Now there is not too many ways to get this done without living next to, or knowing where there is a pond, lake, or a river. Nevertheless, you can always take advantage of when it rains by setting up this next project. You do this by first getting yourself at least three 55 gallons' plastic barrels, or you could use 3 garbage cans. You would spread them out under your gutters on your house, **(if you do not have gutters, I would buy some and plan to put them on)** at lease a ten to fifteen-foot length. Then you would make a round hole along the bottom of the gutter that way when it rains the water will run off your roof and drop down into gutters and then drain out through the holes you have cut in the gutters and into the barrels under the holes.

Now this water will be fine for watering your garden, but if you plan to use it for drinking water, just like the water you would get out of a lake or other sources, it will have to purify it. Now there are several ways to do this, I will suggest two types. By using chemicals, you can buy over the counter, or just by boiling it for at least a 10-minute rolling boil. However, be aware this will only be sufficient to kill off the vast majority of organisms living in the water. It also removes some chemicals by vaporizing them, but it will not remove solids, metals, or minerals. Now you can also use purification tablets or drops. You can purchase these drops or tablets at sporting goods and adventure stores. Keep in mind that this does not taste very good, but protection from bacteria is worth a bitter taste in your mouth. Iodine tablets are the most commonly sold purifying tablets, but you can also use chlorine tablets with the same result. These tablets are most effective when the water you are purifying is 68 degrees F (21 degrees C) or higher. These chemical tablets will kill bacteria living in your water.

Pregnant women, women over 50, and people with thyroid problems or taking Lithium should consult with a doctor before using iodine tablets. First off, strain the water if it has large particles floating around in it. You can do this by pouring the water through a cloth and into the bottle or container that you will be purifying your water. If your tablets or drops came with instructions, follow these now. In general, you will want to use one tablet for each quart or liter of water you wish to purify. Be aware that these tablets generally have an expiration date. If you use them after this date, they are much less likely to be effective. Always check the bottle before using these tablets. Mix the tablets into the water until they dissolve.

Wait 30 minutes before drinking the water, as the tablets need this amount of time to kill any bacteria in the water. You should also be aware that tablets are generally less effective if the water is very cold. If the water is 40 degrees F (4 degrees C), you should wait at least an hour after the tablets have dissolved before drinking the water. You can place the water in the sun to warm it up before using the tablets if you have the time to do so. To lessen the strange taste, the tablets gives the water yon can add flavoring to the water you can use powdered lemonade mix or a pinch of salt will mask the tablet flavor.

FIRE STARTING

One of the most important things that you can learn to do is build a fire, the reason being it will help keep you warm, help keep away predators, cook food, and boil water so it will be safe to drink. When I was a Boy Scout, we learned to make fire by rubbing sticks together, now if you have ever tried this you soon find out how hard this is to do. It is so much easier to do now and not have to try to use sticks. There are numerous ways to build a fire but I will just discuss two of probably the easiest ways. **1. Magnesium Shavings:** You can buy bags or tubes of this on EBay or most stores that sell hiking or camping equipment and it is inexpensive. To begin first try and find a piece of dry tree bark somewhere about the size of an envelope, then either shred up some more bark, dry leaves or small twigs. Make a small pile of these on your piece of bigger tree bark, and then take a clump of Magnesium Shavings about the size of a golf ball and lay this on your shred pile then off to the side of your envelope size of bark have a pile of some medium size twigs. Then you can use a match, lighter, or a Flint Fire Starter to light your pile of Magnesium, then as soon as the pile starts burning take the pile of your medium size twigs and lay it on the fire.

2. Steel Wool: You can buy this at any supermarket or hardware store and it is small enough that you can carry this in your backpack also. You will also need a 9V volt battery, you start out just like you did with the Magnesium, build yourself a bark platform, but now when you put the small twigs, leaves, or small pieces of bark on the platform you will need to tear up pieces of the steel wool and mix it in the pile. Now all you have to do is touch the terminal end of the battery to a spot on the steel wool, and it will take off burning, **(but you do not want to smell and have a lot of the smoke of the of the burning of the steel wool blowing in your face.)** Then when it is burning put a pile of medium size twigs on it just like the Magnesium fire.

APOCALYPSE BUNKERS

I will tell you about four bunkers that we know of, and were set up for doomsdays. However, the chance of getting in one of them will be slim unless you are part of the Government. The first one that I will talk about would probably be your best shot at getting in one.

The Greenbrier Resort: It is located in White Sulphur Springs, West Virginia. It was built in 1958 to house Congress in the event of a nuclear attack, when it was finished in 1961 it was stocked and set-up with survival supplies. It is 720 feet into the hillside and had a power plant, water storage, a pharmacy, and dormitories for more than 1,100 people. Supposedly, the Government no longer uses it since 1992, and the Greenbrier Resort started offering tours of the facility, of course, it no longer has any of the survival supplies left. You can still take a tour of the facility as of this writing.

Site R: The Raven Rock Mountain Complex (RRMC) is an American military installation with an underground nuclear bunker near Blue Ridge Summit, Pennsylvania, at Raven Rock Mountain that serves as an underground Pentagon.

The bunker has emergency operations centers for the United States Army, Navy, and Air Force. It is said to have an entire underground city, complete with streets and pumped in air, and miles of tunnels with access shafts to the surface. Some people say it can sleep up to 3,000 people and even has a presidential apartment. Not much known for sure about this government complex, so your chances of getting in here would be very slim, if not impossible.

Mount Weather: Located in the Blue Ridge Mountains in Bluemont, Virginia about 48 miles from Washington, D.C. The site originally opened as a weather station in the late 1800s. There are two parts: the above ground DEMA complex and the 600,000 square foot underground facility. The aboveground portion of the FEMA complex is at least 434 acres this includes a training area of unspecified size. Area B, the underground complex is said to house sprawling mainframe computers, air circulation pumps, and a television and radio studio for post nuclear presidential broadcasts. Mount Weather has its own leaders, its own police and fire departments, and its own laws. No one is allowed to tour the underground complex. Therefore, your chances of getting near there are very slim seeing how it has armed guards all around the complex.

Capitol Visitor Center: The United States Capitol Visitor Center is a large three level 580,000 square foot building built entirely underground on the east side of the Capitol. It is to be a haven for lawmakers in the event of a disaster. The CVC has space for use by the Congress, including multiple meeting and conference rooms. No one will say for sure if it is protected from bombs, nuclear threats, or biological incidents, but it does have at least four bombproof skylights and a tunnel system large enough for vehicles to get around. The only trouble with this complex is, there is probably no way that a regular citizen could gain access to it seeing how it is in the Capital of the United States

Cheyenne Mountain: Is a triple-peaked mountain in El Paso County, Colorado, southwest of downtown Colorado Springs. The mountain serves as a host for military, communications, recreational, and residential functions. The underground operations center for the North American Aerospace Defense Command (NORAD) built during the Cold War to monitor North American airspace for missile launches and Soviet military aircraft. Built deep within granite, and designed to withstand bombing and fallout from a nuclear bomb. Its function broadened with the end of the Cold War, and then much of its functions transferred to Peterson Air Force Base in 2006. The interior of the mountain became a site for the operations center for the North American Aerospace Defense Command (NORAD).

Its eleven multiple-story buildings stand on coil springs to absorb the shock of a blast, so that up to 800 people could survive fall-out of a nuclear bomb. The facility is behind blast-proof doors. In addition, like all good apocalyptic hideouts it is self-sufficient with its own air system, water, and electricity. It was the "nerve center" for NORAD, they used to offer public tours, but due to security concerns, tours stopped in 1999. Most of the center's operations moved to Peterson Air Force Base in Colorado Springs in 2006, and then in April of 2015 the Pentagon reports that a few operations we will be moving back in. So here is another complex that you would not probably be able to get into seeing how it is a military base.

The main reason I wrote about these bunkers is, that depending what happens in the world to cause the apocalypse it may be worth trying to get to one of these complexes in case the people that have already taken up residency in one of them may be willing to let you join them.

BOOKS

In the first part of my book, I made a list of books that you should buy and keep with you when you bug out. However, I cannot stress how important it is to look at getting one of these books I will talk about now. Seeing how you may not have access to a doctor, I will give you the author's names, but you do not have to buys these particular ones. I have no connection with the people that wrote them I just feel that they work very well for me.

Now if you plan on bugging out and leaving the city wild plants need to become your best friend. They cannot only help feed you they can also help cure most any aliments or injures that you may get. They have been doing this for centuries, before drug; companies started making drugs, if you check into many drugs that are manufactured today, you will find they got their start by using a plant base. If you are a baby boomer like me, your mother probably used some natural home remedies on you when you were growing up. Therefore, you really need to get one of these books or something like them: ***Home Remedies: Herbal***

Remedies: Plants that Heal. Now I bought ***"Encyclopedia of Medicinal Plants, by Andrew Chevallier."*** In addition ***"Nature's Garden a Guide to Identifying and Preparing Edible Wild Plants, by Samuel Thayer."***

Again, I want to thank you for buying my book; I hope this has eased your mind somewhat in preparing for Doomsday. I also am currently writing a science fiction book about time travel called Nazi Time Machine, which I am hoping to have out by late 2016.

Sincerely

Tom Redford